LADYBIRD HISTORIES

ANCIENT GREEKS

History consultant: Philip Parker, historian and author
Map illustrator: Martin Sanders

A catalogue record for this book is available from the British Library

Published by Ladybird Books Ltd
80 Strand, London, WC2R 0RL
A Penguin Company

001

ISBN: 978-0-72329-443-6
Printed in China

ANCIENT GREEKS

Written by Cath Senker
Main illustrations by Emmanuel Cerisier
Cartoon illustrations by Clive Goodyear

CONTENTS

WHO WERE THE ANCIENT GREEKS?

The ancient Greek civilization began around 4,000 years ago and continued for nearly 2,000 years. It disappeared long ago, but we can still visit the remains of Greek buildings and watch Greek plays. Our maths and science teaching theories are based on Greek teachings. So who were the first Greeks?

THE ANCIENT GREEK WORLD

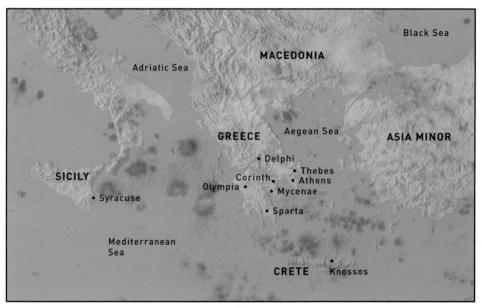

THE RISE OF THE MINOANS

The first civilization in Greece was formed by the Minoans on the island of Crete, around 2000 BCE. They were farmers, and traded around the Mediterranean. The Minoans used writing, but no one knows how to read this early writing now. They were creative people, and made beautiful pots and sculptures. This civilization collapsed around 1450 BCE.

MYCENAEAN CIVILIZATION

The Mycenaean culture arose on the Greek mainland around 1600 BCE. The Mycenaeans traded pottery, cloth and weapons for ivory and metals. They developed a writing system, which archaeologists have learned how to read. From around 1200 BCE, invaders attacked the Mycenaean cities. Bad harvests may have made the situation worse and the Mycenaean cities fell into ruin.

MYCENAEAN DEATH MASK

DARK AGES TO GOLDEN AGE

The period after the fall of the Mycenaean cities is called the Dark Ages of Greece, as there are no written records from that time. Around 800 BCE, the population grew and became wealthier. The Greeks learned ironworking, and made tools for farming and building. They started writing again, and trading. The Golden Age of ancient Greece had arrived.

GREEK SOCIETY

Ancient Greece was formed of many city-states. Each city-state was like a separate little country. The city-state included a city and the land surrounding it. Athens, Sparta, Thebes and Corinth were all city-states. While mostly peaceful, sometimes the city-states fought against each other.

Each city-state developed its own form of rule. Between around 800 and 650 BCE, most Greek states were ruled by an oligarchy – this means 'rule by the few'. A group of rich landowners called aristocrats made all the laws.

TOUGH LAWS

DRACO

In Athens, around 621 BCE, people were unhappy that aristocrats ruled without proper laws. A man called Draco wrote the first set of Athenian laws which were intended to provide a system of justice for all. But his laws were extremely harsh. You could be sentenced to death just for stealing an apple. In the early 500s BCE, Solon changed all the laws (except the law on murder) to make them fairer.

UNDER DRACO'S LAWS, PEOPLE COULD BE PUT TO DEATH EVEN FOR MINOR CRIMES.

TYRANTS

From around 650–500 BCE, city-states were often ruled by one powerful man called a tyrant. This happened when an oligarchy couldn't keep control. Some tyrants ruled well. Around 546 BCE, Peisistratus seized power in Athens and under his rule, the city-state was peaceful and wealthy.

PEISISTRATUS

Life as a slave

The Greeks kept many slaves to do manual work; most were captured in war. Some slaves worked closely with their owners and were well treated, although they had no rights. Others were badly treated, and were beaten or starved. The worst jobs for slaves were working in the silver mines or as oarsmen, rowing a ship. These slaves worked hard all day, never saw the sun and were poorly fed. Many died young.

NEW LANDS, NEW TRADE

Greece was hilly, so it was hard to plant crops. The Greeks needed land for food and they were keen to trade so they could buy goods. So, from around 1050 BCE, adventurous young Greek men sailed away to start colonies in Asia Minor and around the Mediterranean. They did not conquer these lands, but simply settled there. They set up cities that became centres of the Greek language, lifestyle and religion.

TRADING WITH THE LOCALS

Local people mostly welcomed the newcomers, because they bought their spare crops and sold them useful goods. The Greeks exported oil, wine, metalwork, pottery and cloth. They imported grain, spices and salted fish to feed the people back home, as well as papyrus, wood, ivory, precious metals and slaves.

Before the invention of money, people simply exchanged goods. Coins were probably invented at the end of the 600s BCE in Asia Minor and later spread to Greece. Money allowed people to buy or sell without having to swap goods. Each Greek city-state had its own coins, so traders had to visit a money changer when they travelled to another city-state.

GREEK COINS

TRADERS SOLD GOODS AND BOUGHT FOOD AND MATERIALS TO TAKE BACK TO GREECE.

Travel and transport

Greece had few good roads, and most people lived near the sea. The easiest way to transport goods was by boat. Traders travelled between ports on big merchant ships, buying and selling goods. However, they risked the dangers of storms or pirate attacks. For short journeys on land, people used carts pulled by horses, mules, donkeys or oxen to move goods around.

11

ONE MAN, ONE VOTE

As trade increased, craftsmen and traders became wealthier and wanted to have a say in government. They didn't want to be told what to do by one person. Some Greek city-states overthrew their tyrants and brought in a new system of democracy. This gave a wider group of people, both rich and not so rich, a direct say in ruling the city. In Athens, democracy was introduced around 508 BCE, so the citizens helped to rule their city-state.

Only free men over the age of 30 years old were allowed to be citizens. Women, slaves, poor people and foreigners were excluded. Just a small part of the population had a voice in Athenian democracy, but it was a start.

DEMOCRACY IN ACTION

All citizens were members of the Assembly. At least 6,000 citizens had to attend the Assembly to discuss ideas for new laws put to them by the Council. The Council was made up of 500 citizens, chosen by a lottery. Military commanders called *strategoi* carried out the Assembly's decisions. The citizens elected the *strategoi* once a year.

Those accused of crimes were tried at court and by a jury. The accused had to defend themselves; there were no lawyers. Women could not give evidence so men spoke for them. Punishments included fines, being sent away from the city, or even death.

A CRIMINAL IS TAKEN AWAY AFTER HIS TRIAL.

The Parthenon

The most impressive building in Athens was the Parthenon, an elaborate temple. It was built on the Acropolis – a hill overlooking the city. It had columns around the outside and a stone altar at the front for sacrificing animals. A gold and ivory statue more than 12 metres high of the goddess Athena was on display inside. The ruins of the temple remain to this day.

SPARTAN LIFE

Sparta, in the south, was run differently from Athens. The government had two kings, sharing power. An Assembly of Spartan men elected a council of 28 nobles, who decided on policy. Five men called the ephorate controlled the Council, the army and education. They were so powerful that they could stop any Council decision and even overthrow a king.

THE EPHORATE

Sparta did not have slaves but it had workers called *helots* from neighbouring Messenia. The *helots* worked on the land and had to hand over half of their crops to their masters.

WEALTHY LANDOWNERS HAD HELOTS TO DO ALL THE MANUAL LABOUR.

CHILD SOLDIERS

The Spartans did not have much time to enjoy their freedom because they had to join the army. At seven, boys were taken away from their families to start their military training. To toughen them up, they were beaten and left hungry. Boys were encouraged to steal food to make them cunning. Every year, a thrashing competition was held to see who could take the most pain. Some boys died from their wounds.

Men had to marry before the age of 30. If they did not, they were publicly shamed. They had to parade around the *agora* in winter, singing that they had broken the law.

STEALING FOOD WAS PART OF SPARTAN BOYS' MILITARY TRAINING.

Girl athletes

Spartan girls were also taken from their families and trained for fitness, competing in running, wrestling and javelin throwing. They were trained to be fit and strong so they would have healthy babies.

FARMING THE LAND

Many Greeks were farmers. All members of a farming family worked, sometimes with slaves or paid workers. Life was hard – most families only produced enough food for themselves. Farmers planted grain in flat areas and grazed animals on the hillsides. Olive trees and vines grew in the rocky soil.

CROPS

The main crop in ancient Greece was barley. Farmers sowed the grain in autumn to grow over the winter when there was plenty of rain. They harvested it in the spring, and left those fields until the following year to rest and regain goodness.

FARM WORK WAS HARD AND EVEN CHILDREN HAD JOBS TO DO.

The ancient Greeks also grew grapes and harvested them in the autumn. They ate some as fresh fruit and dried some as raisins. Much of the harvest was squeezed to make wine. Some olives were kept for eating, but most were crushed to make oil for cooking and fuel for lamps. Farmers grew many other kinds of fruit and vegetables too, as well as flax to make linen for clothes.

Going to market

Some farmers brought their produce to the *agora* to sell. City people could buy all their food here. Around the *agora* were long open buildings or walkways, called the *stoae*, where traders such as butchers, barbers and cobblers had stalls. Women traded as well as men.

FARM ANIMALS

Greek farmers kept goats and cattle for their milk and hides (skins), and sheep for their wool. They bred pigs and chickens for their meat, and kept bees for their honey. Oxen and mules were useful for pulling ploughs.

THE GREEKS AT HOME

Greek houses were usually quite flimsy and made from mud-brick walls. The walls could be washed away in a big storm. An ancient Greek phrase for burglar translates as 'wall breaker' – it was very easy to break a hole in a Greek house!

OUT IN THE COURTYARD

Houses were built around a central courtyard, with the rooms facing it. In warm weather, people cooked and entertained there, while children and pets played. The altar where the family prayed was in the courtyard, too. Some people were lucky enough to have a well. But most had to fetch water every day from a fountain or natural spring.

THIS VIEW OF A GREEK HOUSE HAS BEEN CUT AWAY TO SHOW THE INSIDE.

FURNITURE FASHIONS

Most Greek homes usually had just a ground floor. Small windows kept the house cool. The floor was simply bare beaten earth or clay. From the 300s BCE, richer homes had pretty mosaics. Walls were sometimes covered with a layer of plaster, painted red or white.

For furniture, the Greeks had couches for sleeping and eating, and low tables with three legs that were easy to balance on the uneven floors. They sat on chairs with cushions or four-legged stools.

HOMES HAD ROOMS FOR EATING AND ENTERTAINING. SOME HOMES HAD SEPARATE ROOMS FOR MEN AND WOMEN.

Going to the toilet

Only rich people had running water in their homes, with toilets linked by clay pipes to drains, which took away waste from the house. Most people used chamber pots and emptied them outdoors, or used a shared outside toilet.

FOOD AND FEASTS

Poor people in ancient Greece ate a simple diet based on bread and porridge. Breakfast was a lump of barley bread soaked in wine. For lunch, people had bread with cheese or with olives and figs. In the evening, they ate barley porridge and vegetables. People drank wine mixed with water, often sweetened with honey. The poorest drank cheap wine, water or goats' milk. There was no tea or coffee in ancient Greece.

The Greeks ate plenty of fruit and vegetables and they loved fish and seafood. People liked to eat fish on a bed of herbs. They had little meat, except at feasts.

WEALTHY GREEKS ENJOYED A VARIED DIET OF MEAT, FISH AND VEGETABLES.

A RICH DIET

Only the wealthy could afford meat. They feasted on birds, including thrushes, nightingales, ducks, geese and quails. They ate grasshoppers, snails and snakes. Desserts included fruit, nuts and honey cakes.

Fish glutton
Fish gluttons stuffed themselves with fish. One writer described a fish glutton who nearly died eating an octopus a metre wide!

Symposiums
Wealthy men held feasts called symposiums, with delicious food and wine. They relaxed on couches and used their fingers to pick food cut up for them by slaves or women. Female musicians played music and danced around them. The guests played board games or *kottabos*, a silly game in which they flicked wine at a target. At more serious symposiums, great philosophers came to discuss their theories.

GREEK FASHION

Most ancient Greeks wore similar clothes whether they were men, women or children, rich or poor. They didn't like to stand out and look different. Everyone wore a loose tunic, which was a long piece of cloth wrapped round the body and held in place with a brooch. Women wore long tunics and men wore short ones. Usually, Greeks didn't wear underwear, so it was bad manners to lift up your tunic in public!

TUNICS AND CLOAKS

The basic tunic was called a *chiton*. Made from a large, rectangular piece of cloth, it was held on the shoulders with buttons or brooches. Women often tied a belt around the waist. In colder weather, they wore a large cloak called a *himation* over the *chiton*.

A man's tunic came down to his thighs. It was sleeveless and fastened on one or both shoulders. Men also wore a *himation*, which they wrapped around the body, throwing the end over one shoulder.

BOTH MEN AND WOMEN WORE TUNICS.

SANDALS AND SHOES

Greeks went barefoot indoors. Outside, people usually wore sandals, swapping them for shoes when the weather grew cold. The poorest people had no footwear at all.

GREEK SANDALS

JEWELLERY

Rich people could afford necklaces, earrings or bracelets made from gold, silver and ivory. Poor people's jewellery was made from bronze, lead, bone or glass. Men often wore a signet ring made of metal such as bronze. This was used to put a seal on documents or goods.

GOLD JEWELLERY

LEAD JEWELLERY

Greek make-up

Greek women loved to wear make-up. They used soot or charcoal to colour their eyebrows or eyelids. Red and green eyeshadows were popular, as was lipstick. Greek women liked to look pale, so they painted their faces with white lead, not knowing that lead was poisonous. Wealthy women spent a long time making themselves look beautiful.

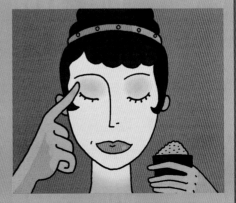

23

CHILDREN IN ANCIENT GREECE

The children of wealthy Greeks stayed at home with their mothers. Poor boys and girls had to go out to work with their parents, and girls helped run the home, too. At the age of seven, boys in Athens started school. Rich girls stayed at home and learned how to cook, weave and make clothes. Spartan children went to military school.

SPARTAN CHILDREN STARTING MILITARY SCHOOL

Baby's first test
When a baby was born, the father checked to see if it looked healthy. If not, it was left outside to die or be rescued and brought up as a slave. Babies that looked strong were kept. A naming ceremony welcomed the infant into the family when it was around ten days old.

TOYS AND GAMES

Wealthy children had plenty of toys, choosing from spinning tops, rocking horses, swings, see-saws, hoops and dolls. They played leapfrog and gave each other piggy-back rides. In one popular game, a child put on a blindfold and had to catch their friends. Children also enjoyed a team game rather like hockey, played with a pig's bladder for a ball.

Children grew up fast. For girls, childhood ended at around fourteen, when their father arranged for them to marry an older man. Before marrying, they had to give up their dolls and take them to the temple. In Athens, boys became adults at eighteen, when they left school and joined the army.

GREEK CHILDREN HAD SIMPLE TOYS TO PLAY WITH.

SCHOOL AND LEARNING

In ancient Greece, only boys went to school. All schools were private, so parents had to pay fees. Poor boys usually went for a few years then started work. Boys from well-off families in Athens went to school from the ages of seven to eighteen. A slave called a *paidagogos* (teacher) went with the boy to school and could beat him if he was naughty!

At school, boys studied maths, reading, writing, poetry and speaking in public. They learned to sing and dance, and to play a musical instrument. Sport was important – the boys spent time boxing, wrestling and running.

BY THE 400s BCE, MOST ATHENIAN CITIZENS COULD READ A LITTLE, AND MANY COULD WRITE.

SCIENCE AT THE GYM

The Greeks also carried on learning as adults. At the *gymnasium* (sports club), as well as exercising, men talked with great philosophers such as Aristotle. They discussed many things, including science and society.

Greek thinkers discovered the principles of maths and science that we still use today. Aristarchus of Samos first suggested that the Earth moved around the Sun. Archimedes worked out how to measure the area of a circle. Pythagoras showed that patterns of numbers can explain how many things work.

ARCHIMEDES

Education for girls

Girls in rich families sometimes had a tutor at home to teach them to read, write and play a musical instrument. Others learned housekeeping. In Hellenistic times (see pages 52–3): schools called *gymnasia* were set up for older boys and girls. These children studied philosophy, books, music, maths and science, and kept fit by doing lots of sport.

FESTIVALS

There were no weekends in ancient Greece. Ordinary people worked every day of the week. They looked forward to festivals because they had a few days off work. Festivals also gave wealthy women a chance to leave the house.

The Greeks had sports and harvest festivals, and religious festivals to honour the gods. They also celebrated weddings and birthdays. Religious festivals were the biggest events. The Greeks believed that if they held festivals to praise the gods, the gods would grant their wishes. Praising the gods might help them to win a war or bring a good harvest.

THE PANATHENAIC FESTIVAL

Festivals were lavish affairs. At the six-day Panathenaic Festival in Athens every four years, the city-state celebrated the goddess Athena's birthday. People enjoyed music, dancing, poetry and sports events. At the end, they joined a huge procession to the Parthenon with gifts for Athena. A robe was draped over her statue, animal sacrifices were offered and a great feast took place.

STATUE OF ATHENA DRAPED IN A ROBE

THE FESTIVAL OF DIONYSUS

At the spring festival for Dionysus, many bulls were sacrificed. The people then sh~~~ ~ meat feast, washed dow~~~ ~~lenty of wine. Over several days, the whole population came to watch plays performed at the theatre.

Music

Music was important to Greek life. It was played at religious festivals, the theatre, weddings and funerals, and to accompany story-telling and poetry readings. Musical instruments included the lyre, a kind of harp, and the aulos, which was like a flute.

FOOD FOR THE FESTIVAL FEAST

SPORT AND THE OLYMPIC GAMES

Sport was important to the Greeks as a part of military training – soldiers needed to be super-fit. The Greeks loved sports contests, which formed part of religious festivals. In Olympia, the competitions developed into the Olympic Games, held to praise the god Zeus. Only men could take part in the Olympic Games. They competed naked, and married women were not allowed to attend.

The first games were held in 776 BCE. They were then held every four years. Wars stopped to allow men from all over Greece to take part. By 472 BCE, the games lasted five days.

LONG JUMP

Pankration
This violent sport was a mix of wrestling and boxing. Biting and gouging out eyes were banned. But it was fine to kick, strangle or jump on an opponent, and break or dislocate his bones.

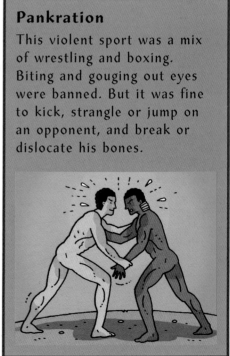

RUNNING, JUMPING AND RACING

A variety of events took place at the games but there were strict rules for each. The pentathlon was a great challenge, involving running, jumping, wrestling, discus and javelin throwing. In another race, runners wore armour. Chariot and horse races were also popular events. Both were extremely dangerous. Up to 40 chariots hurtled around the track, while jockeys rode bareback.

DURING HORSE RACES, RIDERS COULD BE INJURED OR EVEN KILLED.

THE WINNERS

The victors at Olympic events were celebrated as heroes. They received palm branches and a wreath of olive leaves. Successful athletes became professionals who made a living taking part in competitions for their city-state.

GOING TO THE THEATRE

The Greeks loved going to the theatre. Greek theatres were outside and had a semicircle of stone seats for the audience. In the middle was a space called the *orchestra*, a floor where the chorus sang. Behind the *orchestra* was a raised stage for the actors, with doors for them to go on and off stage.

COMEDIES AND TRAGEDIES

By the 400s BCE, the main kinds of plays were comedies and tragedies. Comedies were full of funny stories and rude jokes, and the actors wore bright, cheerful clothes. Satyr plays were the wildest performances, and actors in animal costumes made fun of the people in power. Tragedies were sad and the tragic actors wore dark clothes. Although many characters died, no one saw the deaths on stage.

All the actors were men, who played both the male and female characters. They wore masks to show if they were acting as men or women, and whether they were happy or sad.

CHARACTER MASK

Clever tricks

A hoist behind the stage was used to lift actors from the stage so it looked as if they were flying. Tunnels under the stage allowed actors to disappear, as if by magic.

32

PLAYS

Play-writing competitions were a vital part of religious festivals. Some of the most popular playwrights included Euripides, Aeschylus and Aristophanes.

Plays were extremely long. At the festival for Dionysus in Athens, plays went on from dawn until dusk for several days! But they were very popular – half the people of Athens came along. It was noisy at the theatre. People cheered, booed and argued about the actions on stage.

STONE SEATS WERE UNCOMFORTABLE SO SOME PEOPLE BROUGHT CUSHIONS.

MYTHS AND POETRY

The Greeks loved retelling myths about gods, heroes and monsters. Heroes were nearly as powerful as gods but they could die. They had exciting adventures, with gods and goddesses helping them or causing trouble for them.

GREEK POETRY

Poetry was popular in Greek times. One of the most famous poets was Homer, who may have lived in the 800s BCE. Historians believe he wrote a long poem, called the *Iliad*, about the war with the city of Troy.

One of the greatest poets was Sappho. She was born in about 615 BCE on Lesbos, where women had more freedom than on mainland Greece. Little of her poetry survives.

The Trojan Horse

Later versions of the *Iliad* (written by other authors) described events in the war against Troy. According to legend, the Greeks laid siege to Troy for ten years. The Greeks thought of a trick to seize Troy. They left a huge wooden horse outside the city. The Trojans brought it into the city, thinking it would bring good luck. At night, the Greek soldiers hiding in the horse sneaked out, opened the city gates and let in the Greek army. The soldiers destroyed Troy.

HEROES AND MONSTERS

Heroes often had to fight fierce monsters.

Odysseus killed a cyclops, a giant monster with just one eye.

Hercules was so strong that he killed a lion with his bare hands.

Half man and half bull, the Minotaur lived in the labyrinth.

The brave hero Theseus managed to kill the Minotaur with his sword.

WRITING AND MESSAGES

The Greek alphabet we know today developed from around 800–750 BCE. It had 24 letters and was written from left to right, like English. At first, all the letters were capitals and there were no spaces between the words or commas or full stops. It must have been hard to read!

The city-states all gradually adopted the Greek alphabet so that everyone was using it. This was good for trade and swapping information. Plays, poetry and stories could also then be written down for all to read.

GREEK LETTERS

BOOKS AND WRITING

Slaves had the dull job of copying out books on rolls of papyrus. Papyrus from Egypt was available from the end of the 400s BCE and wasn't expensive. Papyrus didn't always last, so very little Greek writing survives. Examples of Greek writing that have survived to this day, were carved into stone.

At school, children wrote on tablets – wooden boards coated with wax. The tablets were cheap and easy to make. The children scratched their letters into the wax with a sharp metal stick called a stylus. When they had finished, they smoothed over the wax and reused it.

PRACTISING WRITING ON TABLETS

Spreading the news

The Greeks had interesting ways of sending messages: they trained pigeons to carry messages. They set fires on top of mountains to send smoke signals to another city-state. Long-distance runners were also commonly used. For example, in 490 BCE, Athens was at war with Persia. The armies fought at the Battle of Marathon, and the Greeks won. They sent back a message to Athens with a runner. The distance was about 24 miles. The modern marathon, a race of just over 26 miles, got its name from this run.

GODS AND GODDESSES

The Greeks believed in a vast number of gods and goddesses. They thought that the gods had power over everything. Zeus was the leader of the gods. Aphrodite was the goddess of love, Ares the god of war and Poseidon god of the sea. Hades ruled the Underworld, the Kingdom of the Dead.
The Greeks thought the gods were like humans in that they fought, loved and had children. Except they never died.

WORSHIPPING THE GODS

The Greeks wanted to keep their gods happy so they would keep them safe from danger and bring them good luck. People often prayed to the gods at an altar at home and at the temple.

Advice from the oracle

People visited an oracle at a temple to find out what the future held. People believed the gods spoke through the oracle, who was a priest or priestess. At Corinth, the priest lay in a secret tunnel under the altar to speak his answers, pretending to be the god himself!

Each temple had a statue of a god. People believed that the spirit of the god was inside the statue, so they offered it special gifts. At big festivals, they sacrificed animals. They thought that the gods preferred fat and bones, so people could enjoy the tasty meat!

BRINGING A COW
TO BE SACRIFICED

Greek priests looked for omens in the guts of sacrificed animals – signs that they believed could foretell the future. They checked for omens before important events, such as going into battle. If a sacrificed animal had a healthy liver, this meant they would beat their enemies.

39

TEMPLES AND PUBLIC BUILDINGS

The Greeks lived in simple homes, but they built impressive temples all over Greece and the colonies. From the late 500s BCE, they constructed elegant public buildings, too. Greek workers spent many years working hard under the hot sun to complete these beautiful masterpieces of architecture.

In early Greek times, temples were built with mud bricks. Later, builders used long-lasting stone. They hauled the blocks of stone in carts to the site. Stone workers shaped them with hammers and chisels. Workers used ropes and pulleys to lift the heavy stones, and levers to move them into place. Once in position, they polished them. Then they added the wooden roof frame and ceiling.

BUILDING A HOUSE

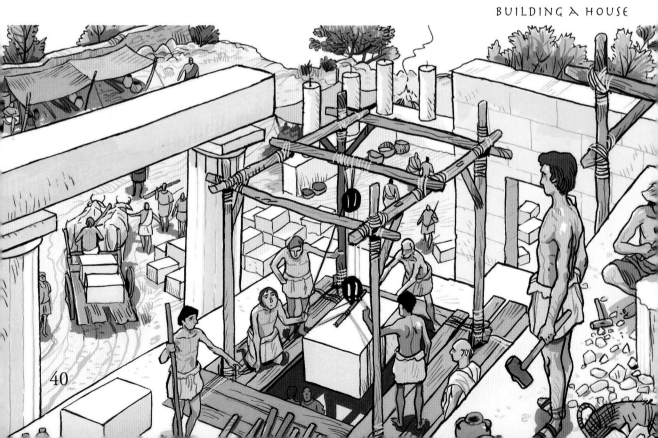

40

FROM DORIC TO CORINTHIAN

Temple styles changed over time as workers' skills improved. The early Doric columns that held up roofs had a simple, thick design, with a plain capital (top). Ionic columns were more slender, with scrolls on the capitals. Corinthian columns were detailed with acanthus leaves.

DORIC

IONIC

CORINTHIAN

PUBLIC BUILDINGS

By the 400s BCE, the Greeks planned towns in neat squares, with areas for different activities. Public buildings included the *agora* and the *stoae*, and special buildings for the government. The Council met in the *bouleterion* (Council house). The Top Council committee met in a round building called a *tholos*.

A GREEK TOWN CENTRE

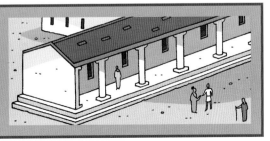

The *stoa*
The long, narrow *stoa* had a covered walkway along the side to provide shelter from the sun and rain. People gathered here to discuss business and talk to their friends.

ARTS AND CRAFTS

Sculpture, painting and pottery were very important in ancient Greece. Sculptures honouring the gods changed in style over time from stiff-looking forms to more life-like figures. We can still see some examples of sculpture and pottery, but no Greek paintings have survived.

Making bronze

The Greeks made statues, jugs and mirrors from bronze. First, they heated copper and tin until they melted and formed bronze. Then, they poured the liquid metal into a mould to give the shape of the object, and left it to cool and become solid.

To make realistic sculptures, Greek sculptors used athletes as models. Athletes wore no clothes so the artists could see the detail of their bodies. Sculptors created their works from marble or limestone and painted them in bright colours.

POTTERY PATTERNS

Craft workers made clay vases, plates and bowls, decorated with paintings of daily life. The best pottery was from Athens. The local clay turned an attractive reddish-brown when it was baked in the kiln. Athenian pottery was sold all over the Greek world.

Like sculpture, pottery patterns changed over time. From the 900s to the 600s BCE, patterns with shapes were popular. In the 500s BCE, black figures were painted on the background. From about 500 BCE, the colours were switched. The figures were reddish-brown, and the background was black.

IF A POT BROKE WHILE BEING MADE, THE DEMON 'SYNTRIPS' (HIS NAME MEANT 'SMASHER') GOT THE BLAME!

PRECIOUS PRODUCTS

Metal workers used gold and silver to make coins, jewellery and luxury goods. Some statues were even made of gold. Few have survived – the precious metals were mostly melted down and reused.

BRONZE IS SHINY AND YELLOW WHEN FIRST CAST, BUT TURNS GREEN OVER TIME.

DOCTORS AND DISEASE

The early Greeks thought that getting a disease was a terrible punishment from the gods. They prayed for a cure. Priests carried out treatments, often using herbal remedies. From the 400s BCE, however, doctors used science to find cures – and these were then used for hundreds of years.

DIET, EXERCISE AND TREATMENT

HIPPOCRATES

The doctor Hippocrates taught people to stay healthy by eating a good diet and taking exercise. He and other doctors discovered treatments we now know are helpful. Hippocrates told patients to chew willow bark to reduce fevers and swelling. A chemical in willow bark is still used to treat pain today.

Some treatments were painful and less helpful. Doctors removed blood from the body because they believed it contained disease. They used a hot cup to draw blood from a wound as it cooled, or used leeches to suck the blood out. Some treated slipped discs by standing on the patient's back.

Ancient Greek experiments

Hippocrates did experiments to learn about the body. He took substances such as ear wax and vomit and tested them by tasting them. Yuck! Herophilus (335–280 BCE) cut up the bodies of criminals to find out what was inside.

DOCTORS USED HERBS AND PLANTS TO MAKE MEDICINES.

SURGERY

Some surgeons in Greek times were very skilled. They could set broken bones, cut off a badly diseased limb and dress wounds. They also pulled out rotten teeth. Surgery was extremely dangerous though. There was nothing to stop the pain and wounds often became infected, killing the patient.

TEETH WERE PULLED OUT WITHOUT ANAESTHETIC.

SURGICAL TOOLS

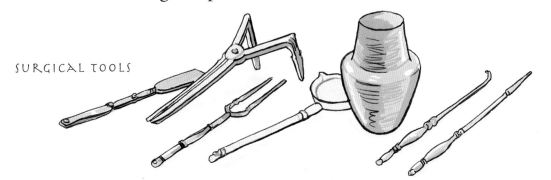

SOLDIERS IN BATTLE

The Greek city-states sometimes fought each other, as well as other countries. So they all kept well-trained armies. In Athens, from about 330 BCE, men had to join the army for two years when they were eighteen. In Sparta, boys trained as soldiers from the age of seven.

HOPLITES

Most fighters were *hoplites*, or foot soldiers. They had to buy their own weapons and armour. They had a shield to protect them and wore a helmet, usually made of bronze, to cover the whole head and the back of the neck. A breastplate covered the chest, and soldiers wore leg guards called greaves. Poorer citizens did not serve as *hoplites* but were still called up into the army in an emergency. They went into battle with just a bow and arrow or a slingshot for throwing stones.

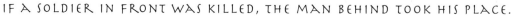

IF A SOLDIER IN FRONT WAS KILLED, THE MAN BEHIND TOOK HIS PLACE.

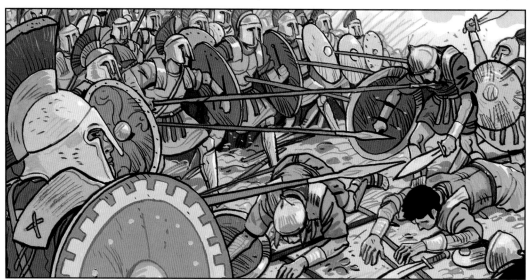

HOW BATTLES WERE FOUGHT

On land, the two armies rushed at each other and fought hand to hand. Soldiers struck at enemies with spears or jabbed with a sword. The weapons clashed loudly and many were wounded or killed.

SIEGE!

Armies sometimes put an enemy city-state under siege. They attacked the city walls with battering rams and rocks fired from giant catapults. The defenders struck back – sometimes they dropped boiling water or hot sand on their enemies' heads from above.

HOT SAND WAS POURED DOWN ON THE ENEMIES' HEADS.

Sea battles

Some city-states had large navies, and big battles were often fought at sea. The *trireme* was the fastest battleship. Rowed by 170 oarsmen, it had a ram for smashing enemy ships. Once they had rammed an enemy ship, the archers fired at the crew.

THE GREEKS AT WAR

The most important wars included the war against Persia (490–479 BCE) and the Peloponnesian War (431–404 BCE). The Persian War broke out when Persian-occupied Greek city-states tried to throw off their rule. The Peloponnesian War was a power struggle between Athens and Sparta.

In 490 BCE, Darius I of Persia attacked Greece. At the Battle of Marathon, there were far fewer Athenian soldiers but they won the battle because they had better tactics.

PUSHING OUT THE PERSIANS

In 480 BCE, the Persians struck again under King Xerxes. They attacked Athens and completely destroyed the city.

THE PERSIAN WARS

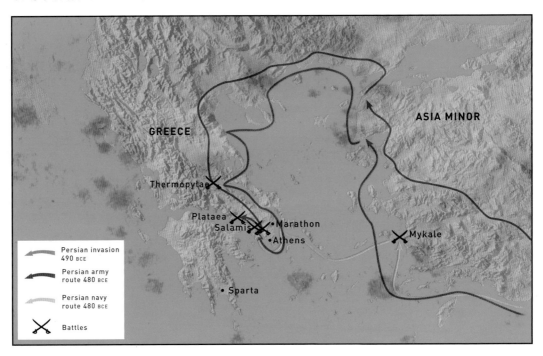

GREECE

ASIA MINOR

Thermopylae

Plataea
Salamis •Marathon
•Athens

Mykale

• Sparta

Persian invasion
490 BCE

Persian army
route 480 BCE

Persian navy
route 480 BCE

Battles

The Greeks fought back and defeated the Persians at the battles of Salamis and Plataea, pushing the Persian forces out of Greece. Athens was rebuilt and, for a time, became the most successful Greek city-state.

GREEK AND
PERSIAN
SOLDIERS

THE PELOPONNESIAN WAR

During this war, Athens and Sparta both formed alliances with other city-states. Athens had a better navy. The Spartan army, with its highly trained soldiers, was hard to beat. So the Athenians avoided fighting Sparta on land, and stayed within the city walls. The Spartans laid siege to Athens, and for a long time, no one could win. In the end, Athens gave in and Sparta won. Sparta became the greatest Greek power.

SOLDIERS IN THE PELOPONNESIAN WAR

Xerxes' bridge

In 480 BCE, King Xerxes of Persia needed to move his army to Greece so he built a bridge between the two countries. When a storm smashed it, he was incredibly angry!

ALEXANDER THE GREAT

ALEXANDER
THE GREAT

By the 300s BCE, Greece was no longer a mighty power. In 338 BCE, Philip II, the leader of Macedonia, defeated all the Greek city-states, and they became subject to Macedonian rule. Two years later, Philip's son Alexander became ruler. He was determined to conquer Persia and expand his empire. In just eleven years, from 334–323 BCE, Alexander created the largest empire the ancient world had ever seen.

ALEXANDER THE GREAT'S EMPIRE

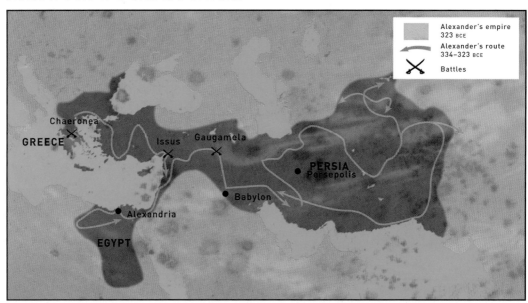

Alexander's empire
323 BCE

Alexander's route
334–323 BCE

Battles

Chaeronea
GREECE
Issus
Gaugamela
PERSIA
Persepolis
Babylon
Alexandria
EGYPT

Living tanks

When Alexander invaded India, his army faced 'living tanks' – enormous elephants carrying archers firing arrows. But Alexander kept his forces in a tight block and the elephants couldn't pass through.

MARCHING THROUGH ASIA

First, Alexander beat the Persians at the Battle of Issus (in modern-day Turkey), in 333 BCE. Then, in 331 BCE, he crushed them at Gaugamela, which is now present-day Iraq. Continuing to march, he took Persepolis, the Persian capital and conquered Syria, Egypt, Afghanistan and Iran. Alexander founded around 70 new cities, naming many of them after himself. He even named one city after his favourite horse, Bucephalus.

ALEXANDER WAS ONLY TWENTY WHEN HE BECAME RULER.

SUDDEN DEATH

In 326 BCE Alexander began to march through India. But after eight years of fighting, his main force of Macedonian soldiers refused to go another step. So Alexander turned towards home. Upon reaching Babylon in 323 BCE, he was taken ill and died. He was only thirty-two.

Alexander the Great had a huge impact on the ancient world. Greek people stayed behind in all the areas he conquered, so Greek influence continued well after his death.

THE END OF THE EMPIRE

The period between Alexander's death and about 100 BCE is usually called the Hellenistic Age – the name comes from *hellene*, the Greek word for 'Greek'. Different empires were in power during this time but the Greek language, culture and building style continued to spread in western Asia. Yet Greece itself was no longer the centre of this culture.

THE RISE OF THE ROMANS

A new empire was rising in the West. In Italy, the Romans grew stronger. By 250 BCE, they controlled most of the country and then their empire began to expand further.

THE ROMAN EMPIRE 44 BCE

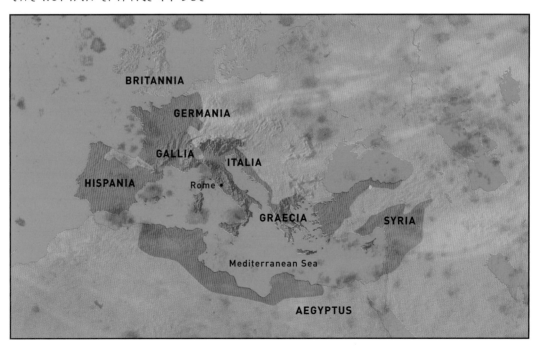

The Romans gradually conquered all the Hellenistic kingdoms. In 146 BCE, Greece became a province of the Roman Empire, although Athens remained an important city with some freedom from the Romans. In 30 BCE, Egypt, the very last Greek-ruled kingdom of Alexander's empire, came under Roman control. However, the Romans adopted much of Greek culture and spread it across their huge empire. Greek writings, philosophy, art and science were kept alive across the ancient world for many years to come.

Archimedes' death rays

One story says that in 211 BCE, scientist Archimedes developed a weapon to stop the Romans from invading his city, Syracuse. He built giant mirrors to reflect the sun on to Roman ships entering the harbour. The rays were so hot that they set the ships on fire. However, the Romans eventually broke through, and Archimedes was killed.

WHAT THE ANCIENT GREEKS DID FOR US

So much of ancient Greek culture is still with us today. Some common English words come from Greek, such as 'alphabet' and 'athlete'. We still read many ancient Greek stories. Greek designs are found in buildings, paintings and sculpture. Edinburgh in Scotland is known as the 'Athens of the North' because of its many Greek-influenced buildings.

THE NATIONAL MONUMENT AT CALTON HILL, EDINBURGH

The Olympic Games

The modern Olympic Games began in 1896. Some events are similar to those in ancient times. We still have running races, although we no longer have a race in which athletes wear armour! Wrestling also still exists, although the rules are much stricter now.

IDEAS ABOUT SCIENCE

Much of what we know today about maths and science is based on principles discovered by the ancient Greeks. Pythagoras worked out how the strings of a musical instrument make a pleasant sound. He discovered that if you know the length of two sides of a right-angled triangle, you can find the third side. Firefighters can use this to work out how long a ladder they need to rescue someone high up in a burning building.

FIREFIGHTERS

CARING FOR THE SICK

Doctors still swear the Hippocratic Oath, a modern version of a Greek promise to protect patients from harm. Hippocrates is seen as the father of modern medicine. He told doctors to look carefully at patients every day and note any changes. This is still done in hospitals today.

DOCTOR

DEMOCRACY

Many countries are ruled by a democracy. People can vote for their government and have a say in how the country is run.

POLITICIANS

55

WHO'S WHO

Archimedes (c.287–212 BCE)

Archimedes was a scientist, mathematician and inventor, born in Syracuse, Sicily. He worked out how to use a lever and how to measure circles. A device for raising water was named after him. He was killed by the Romans invading Syracuse.

Aristarchus (c.310–230 BCE)

Aristarchus was an astronomer. He was the first person to suggest that the Earth moved around the Sun (not the other way round). Aristarchus worked out the relative size of the Sun compared to the Earth and the distance between them.

Aristotle (384–322 BCE)

A philosopher from Athens, he taught Alexander, the son of Philip II of Macedonia. He returned to Athens in 335 BCE and set up a school. Aristotle devised the first classification of animals and he invented logic, the science of reasoning.

Alexander the Great (356–323 BCE)

In 336 BCE, Alexander became king of Macedonia. Under his command, the Macedonian army defeated the Persian Empire, and took control of a vast area of Asia. He created the biggest empire in the ancient world. He died of a fever, aged just 32.

Draco (600s BCE)

Draco made a harsh set of laws in Athens in about 621 BCE. All crimes were punished with death. The ruler Solon changed Draco's laws in the early 500s BCE. Today, we still call a tough rule 'draconian' after Draco.

Herophilus (c.335–280 BCE)

Often known as the father of anatomy, Herophilus was a doctor in Alexandria, Egypt. He cut up dead bodies to study what lay inside. He studied the brain and other organs and described them carefully. He was the first person to measure the pulse – the beat of blood as it moves round the body.

Hippocrates (*c.*460–*c.*375 BCE)

Hippocrates is thought of as the father of medicine. He travelled widely in Greece and Asia, working as a doctor and teaching medicine. Hippocrates wrote many works about diseases, medicines and how to treat wounds and set broken bones.

Homer (*c.*800s or 700s BCE)

Historians believe that Homer was a blind poet, possibly from the island of Chios, who moved from place to place, speaking his poetry. He wrote two long poems, the *Iliad* and the *Odyssey*, which retell ancient Greek myths. Many experts believe that the poems were not written by one person.

Peisistratus (died 527 BCE)

Peisistratus gained power in Athens by force. But he kept Athens at peace, so trade and industry could grow. He spent money on festivals and improving the water supply and lent money to farmers to help them grow more crops. His rule was seen as a Golden Age for Athens.

Philip II (382–336 BCE)

Philip II started ruling Macedonia in 359 BCE. He was a great leader who conquered land for Macedonia. He married Olympias and they had a son, Alexander. Philip was killed in 336 BCE – possibly by poison. Some historians think that Olympias and Alexander plotted his murder.

Pythagoras (*c.*590–*c.*500 BCE)

Pythagoras founded a school in Croton, Southern Italy. He believed that maths could explain the natural world. Pythagoras developed many mathematical ideas, for example, how musical notes sound pleasant together and the mathematics of triangles.

Sappho (born *c.*612 BCE)

Born on the island of Lesbos, Sappho probably moved to Sicily. Historians believe that she wrote ten books of poetry but only one complete poem still exists. Sappho wrote about the loves and hates of wealthy women. It was rare for a woman at that time to become famous for her skills.

TIMELINE

2000 BCE	The Minoans, on Crete, form the first Greek civilization
1600 BCE	The Mycenaean civilization begins
1450 BCE	Minoan civilization collapses
1100 BCE	The Mycenaean civilization dies out
1100–800 BCE	The Greek Dark Ages – the population falls and writing stops
1050 BCE	The Greeks start to found colonies in Asia Minor
800–650 BCE	Most Greek city-states are run by an oligarchy
900s to 600s BCE	Pottery patterns with shapes are popular
800s BCE	Homer writes his poems, the *Iliad* and the *Odyssey* (although modern historians think he was probably not the only writer)
800–750 BCE	The Greek alphabet develops
776 BCE	The first Olympic Games take place at Olympia
750–650 BCE	Greeks establish colonies around the Mediterranean
621 BCE	In Athens, Draco writes harsh laws for the city-state
650–500 BCE	City-states are often ruled by a tyrant
End 600s BCE	Money is invented in Asia Minor and soon spreads to Greece
546 BCE	Peisistratus seizes power in Athens and rules as a tyrant
508 BCE	Athens brings in democracy
End of 400s BCE	Papyrus becomes available
490–479 BCE	War between Greece and Persia

490 BCE	The Battle of Marathon between the Greeks and the Persians
480 BCE	The Persians beat the Greeks at the Battle of Thermopylae. The Persians destroy the city of Athens
472 BCE	By now, the Olympic Games lasts for five days
400s BCE	Athens is the most powerful city-state
431–404 BCE	The Peloponnesian War between Athens and Sparta
338 BCE	Philip II of Macedonia defeats all the Greek city-states
336 BCE	Alexander the Great becomes King of Macedonia
334–323 BCE	Alexander expands the Macedonian empire
333 BCE	Alexander beats the Persians at the Battle of Issus (now Turkey)
335–280 BCE	Herophilus cuts up the bodies of dead criminals to look inside
331 BCE	Alexander defeats the Persians at Gaugamela, in present-day Iraq
326 BCE	Alexander marches his troops to India but then turns back
300s BCE	Rich people start using mosaics on their floors
323 BCE	Alexander falls ill in Babylon and dies, aged 32
300s–c.30 BCE	The Hellenistic Age: Greek culture is still important in western Asia
211 BCE	Archimedes' 'death rays' said to stop Roman ships from invading Syracuse
146 BCE	Greece becomes a province of the Roman Empire
30 BCE	Egypt comes under Roman rule

GLOSSARY

agora a space in a city-state with a market

altar a place for offering gifts to a god or goddess

aristocrat a member of a rich Greek family that owned lots of land

Assembly a group of citizens (only men) who decided how the country was run

astronomer someone who studies the stars and night sky

chariot an open cart with two wheels

chisel a tool for shaping wood, stone or metal

chorus a group of men who spoke together in plays and sang or danced

citizen a man over 30 who was born in a city-state and could take part in the government

city-state a city with land around it that was ruled like a country

civilization the way of life of a group of people from one area

colonies settlements overseas of people from another country, governed by that country

democracy a system of government. The citizens can vote to elect the people who run it

discus a heavy, flat, round object thrown in a sporting event

empire a group of countries run by one country

export	to sell goods to another country
foretell	to know or say what will happen, especially by using magic powers
grapevine	a climbing plant that produces grapes
gymnasium	a place where people trained in athletics. People studied there, too
Hellenistic	to do with the history, language and culture of Greece from the 300s to about 30 BCE
import	to buy goods from another country
ironworking	making things from iron, such as parts of buildings or weapons
javelin	a light spear (long stick with a pointed end), which is thrown in a sporting event
jury	members of the public who listen to a court case and decide whether somebody is guilty
kiln	a large oven for baking clay and bricks
labyrinth	a maze-like structure made to hold the Minotaur
merchant ship	a ship used for carrying goods to trade
money changer	a person who changes money from one kind to another to allow people to trade
mosaic	a picture or pattern made by arranging pieces of glass or stone of different colours
mould	a hollow container used to give shape to hot liquid material when it cools and hardens

myth	an ancient story which may be based on something that actually happened
oligarchy	a government in which a small group of people hold all the power
omen	a sign of what is going to happen
oracle	a place where people could go to ask the gods for information about the future
papyrus	paper made from the grass-like papyrus plant
pulley	a wheel over which a rope or chain is pulled in order to lift or lower heavy objects
sacrifice	an offering to a god, especially an animal that has been killed in a special way
sculpture	a work of art that is a solid figure or object made by shaping metal, stone or clay
siege	the surrounding of a town by an enemy army, which stops the supply of food reaching the people inside
slave	a person who is owned by another person and is forced to work for them
spirit	the part of a person or god to do with their mind and feelings rather than their body
spring	a place where water comes out of the ground
symposium	a feast for wealthy men
temple	a building used for the worship of a god
tyrant	a ruler who overthrew existing kings or oligarchs and held absolute power

PLACES TO VISIT

Museums in the UK

Ashmolean Museum of Art and Archaeology, Oxford

Birmingham Museum and Art Gallery, Birmingham

The British Museum, London

Manchester Museum, University of Manchester

World Museum, Liverpool

Sites in Greece

The Acropolis, Athens

Delphi

Epidaurus

Olympia

Sparta

Sites in other countries

Paestum, Italy

Troy, Turkey

Valley of the Temples, Sicily

INDEX